The Little Lost Lamb

by Ruth Shannon Odor
illustrated by Diana Magnuson

THE CHILD'S WORLD

ELGIN, ILLINOIS 60120

Library of Congress Cataloging in Publication Data

Odor, Ruth Shannon.
 The little lost lamb.

 (Bible story books)
 SUMMARY: A retelling of the New Testament parable of the lost sheep.
 1. Lost sheep (Parable)—Juvenile literature.
 [1. Lost sheep (Parable).   2. Parables.
 3. Bible stories—N.T.]   I. Magnuson, Diana.
 II. Title.   III. Series.
 BT378.L6033   226'.2'09505   79-13155
 ISBN 0-89565-088-6

Distributed by Standard Publishing, 8121 Hamilton Avenue, Cincinnati, Ohio 45231.

© 1979 The Child's World, Inc.
All rights reserved. Printed in U.S.A.

The Little Lost Lamb

The Biblical account of this story
is found in *Matthew 18:12-14* and *Luke 15:3-7*.

Once there lived a shepherd. The shepherd had one hundred sheep. Early each morning, the shepherd opened the gate of the sheepfold and led his sheep out to the fields.

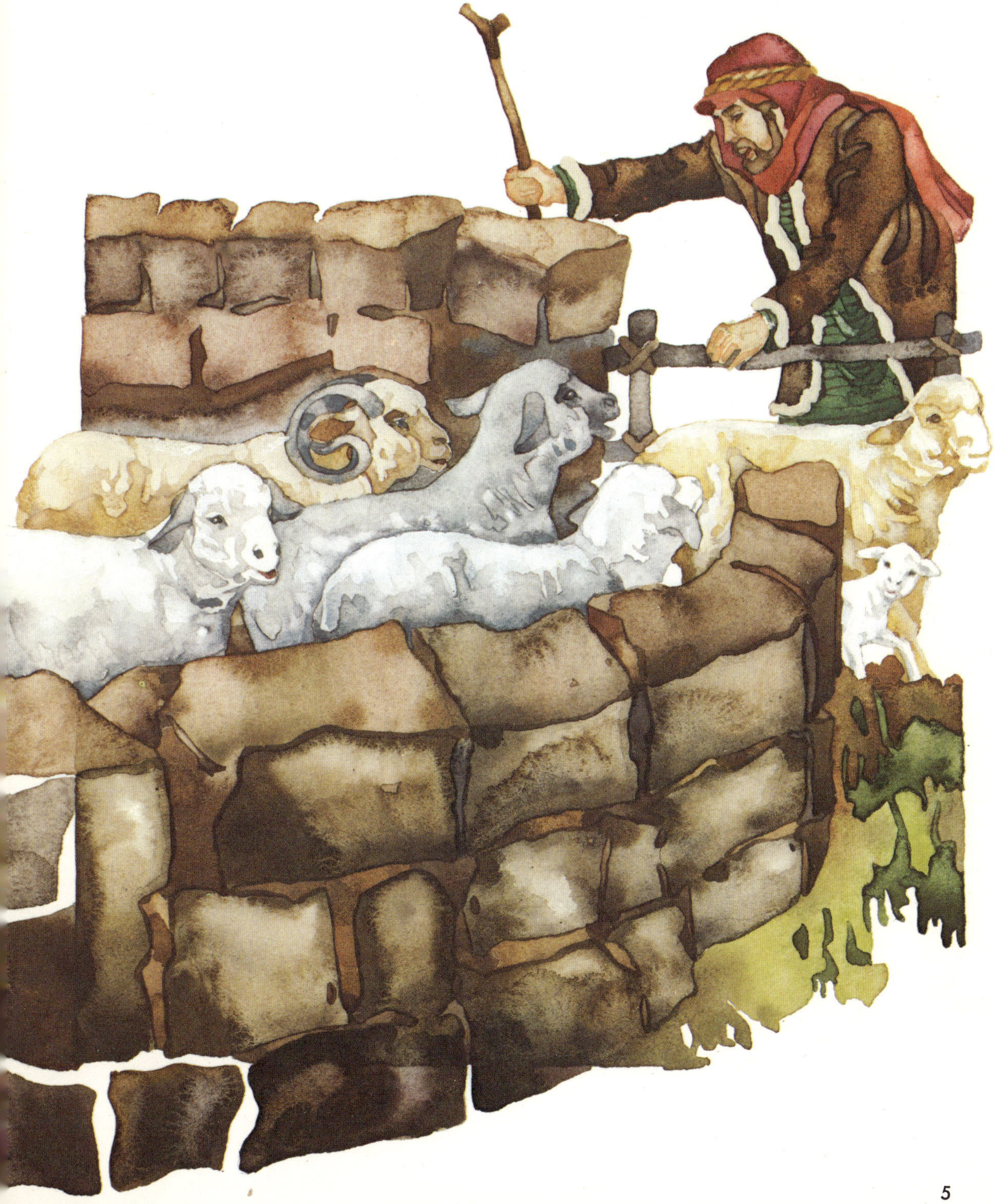

There were big sheep and little sheep and middle-sized sheep. There were mother sheep with little lambs. All of them followed the shepherd as he walked along the path.

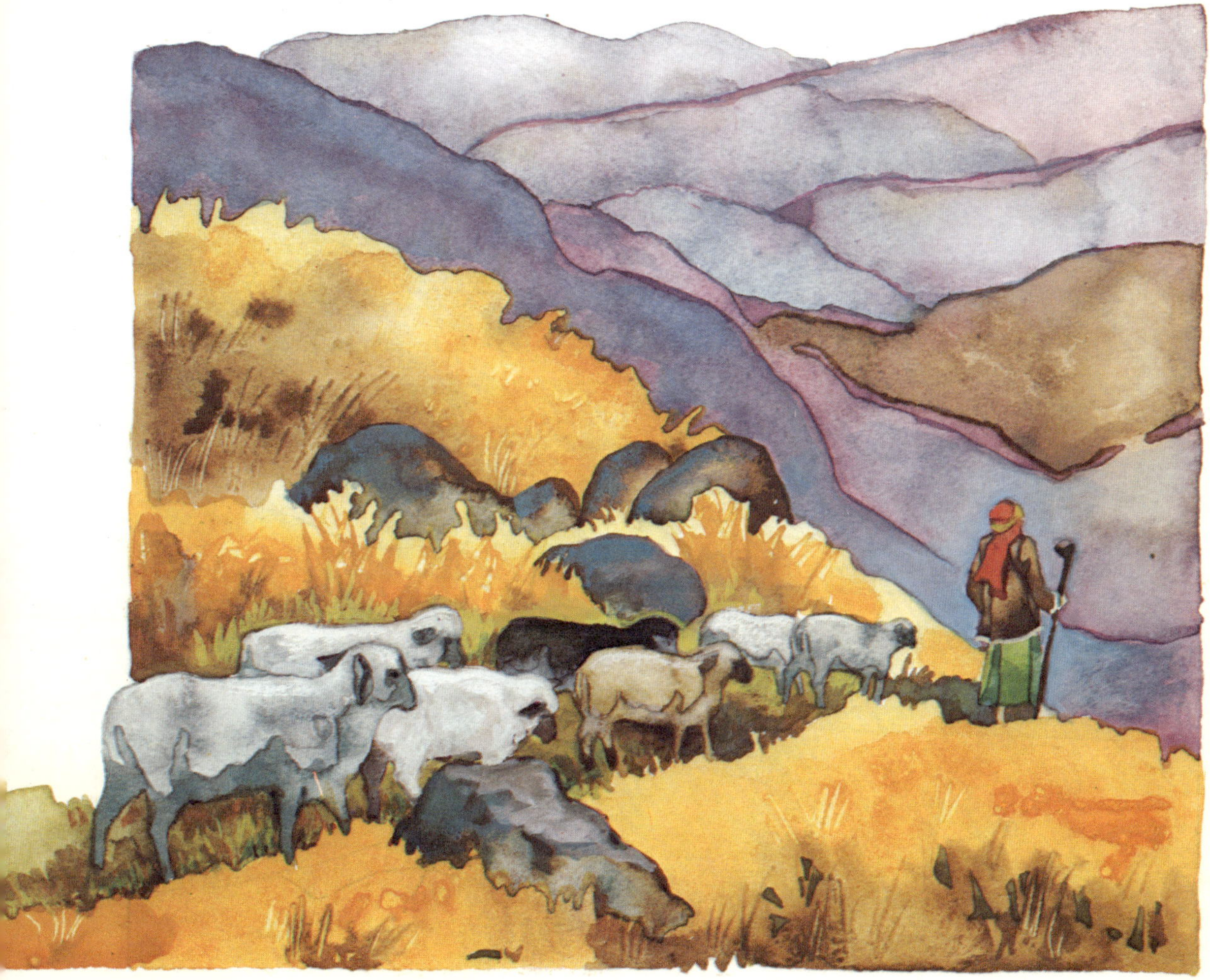

Out in the fields, the sheep ate the crisp, green grass. They rested in shady places beside cool, still water.

The shepherd loved his sheep. He knew each one — the big ones, the little ones, the middle-sized ones. He knew the mother of each little lamb.

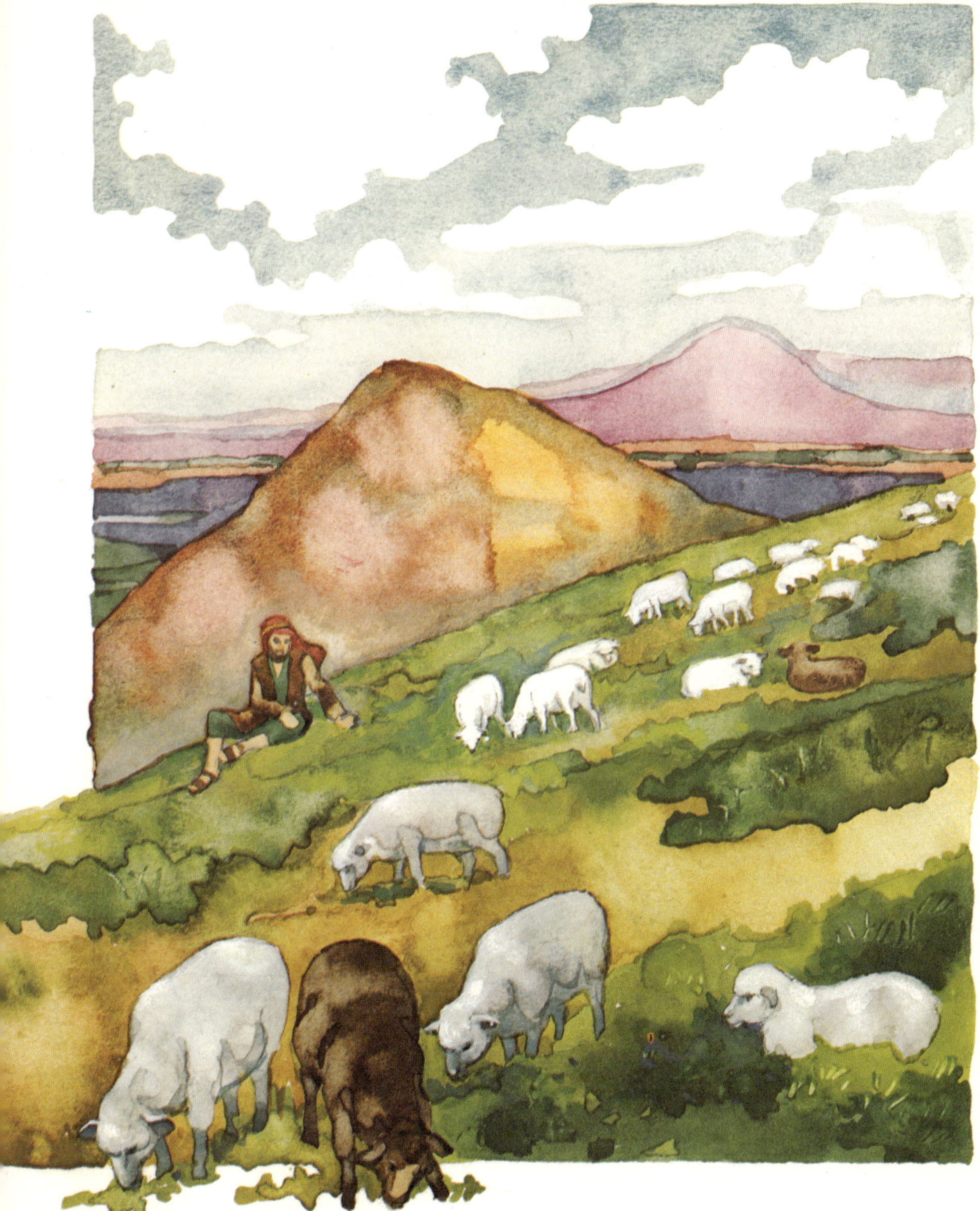

The shepherd took good care of his sheep. He led them to places where there was lots of crisp, green grass to eat and cool, still water to drink and tall, green trees under which to rest.

Sometimes, the shepherd led the sheep over rocky places. He watched to see that nothing hurt his sheep. He watched for snakes. He watched for lions and bears.

11

Each evening, the shepherd led his sheep back to the sheepfold. There they could sleep safely through the night. Each evening, he counted his sheep to be sure that all of them were there.

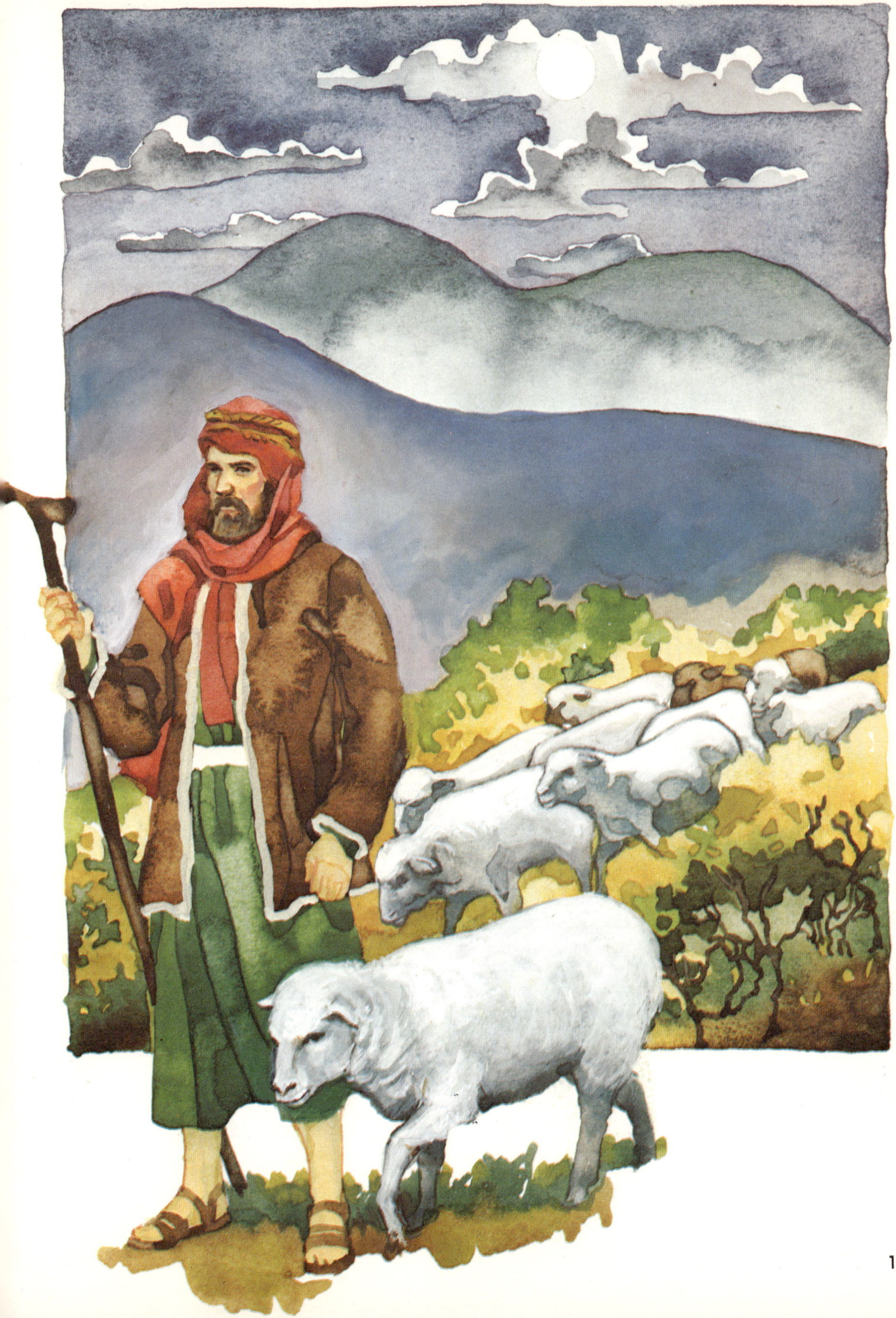

One evening, the shepherd did not count 100 sheep! He counted only 99!

"I must have counted wrong," he said. And he counted once again. "One, two, three, four, five..." and on to, "95, 96, 97, 98, 99..." There were only 99 sheep! One was not there! One was lost! Which one was it?

It was...yes...it was one of the mother sheeps' little lambs! A little lamb was lost!

"I must find my little lamb," said the shepherd. He fastened the gate of the sheepfold. He began the long walk back to the field.

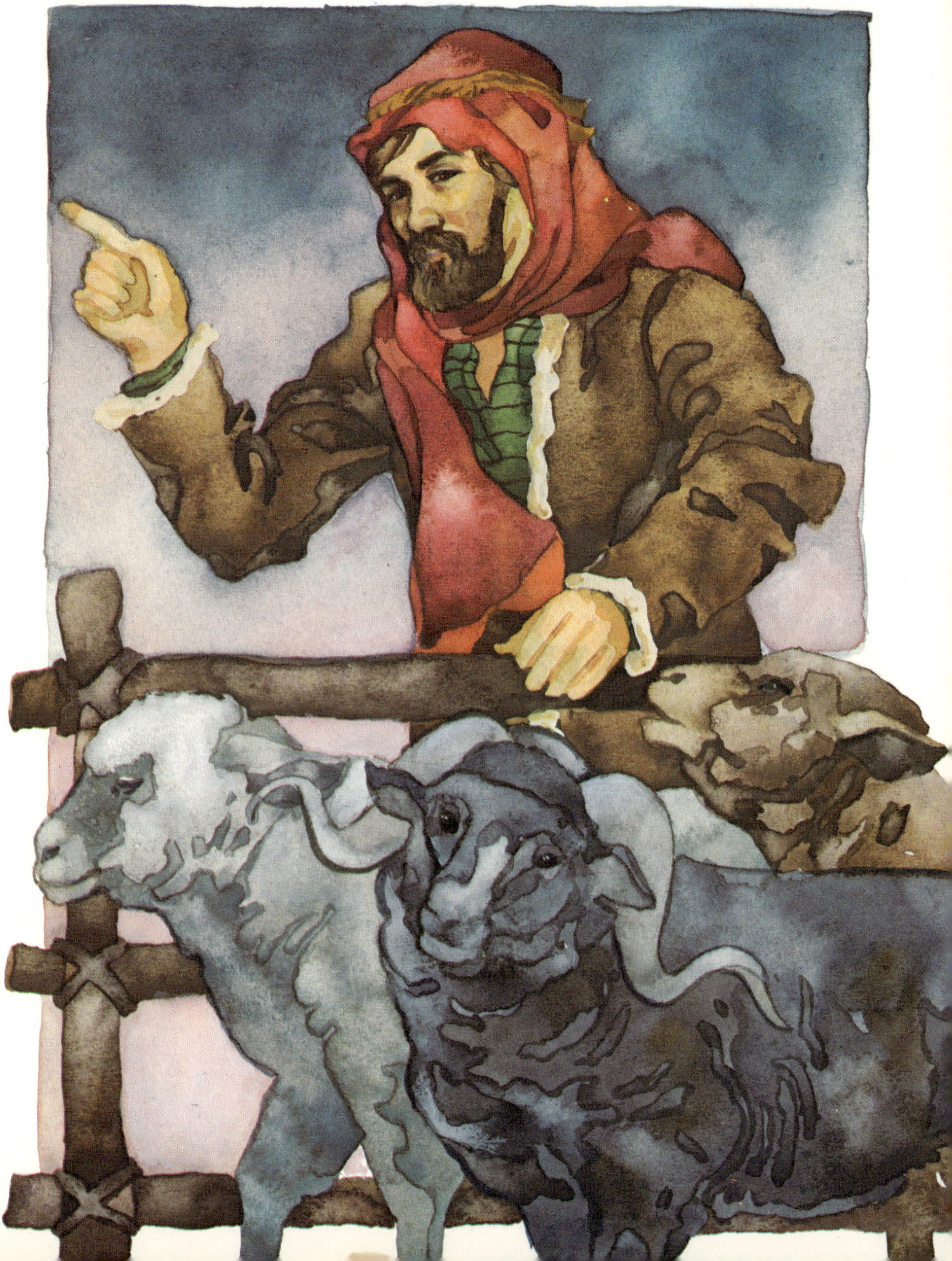

Night had come. And the night was dark and cold. The shepherd wrapped his cloak more tightly around him. He looked carefully to find the path.

On and on he walked — all the way to the field. He called and called. "My sheep know my voice," he said. "If my little lost lamb hears me, he will answer."

The shepherd stopped to listen. But there was no sound — no "Baa, baa" that he wanted so much to hear.

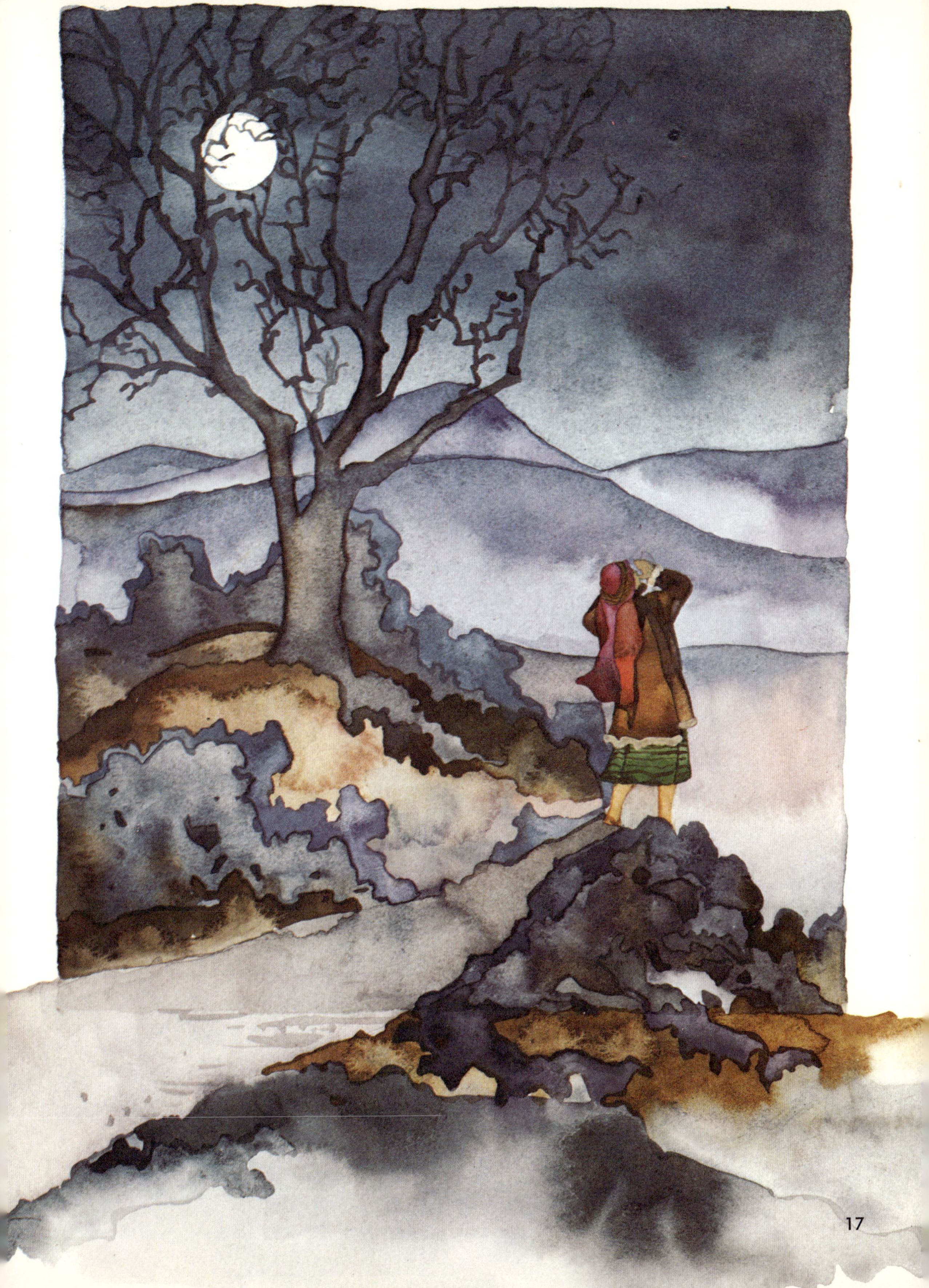

"That lamb wandered away today," said the shepherd. "Perhaps he chased a butterfly or ran to see what was on the other side of a big rock. Then he was lost and could not find us. Oh, I wonder where you are, dear little lamb. Are you hurt? Are you afraid?"

And once again, the shepherd called. But there was no answer.

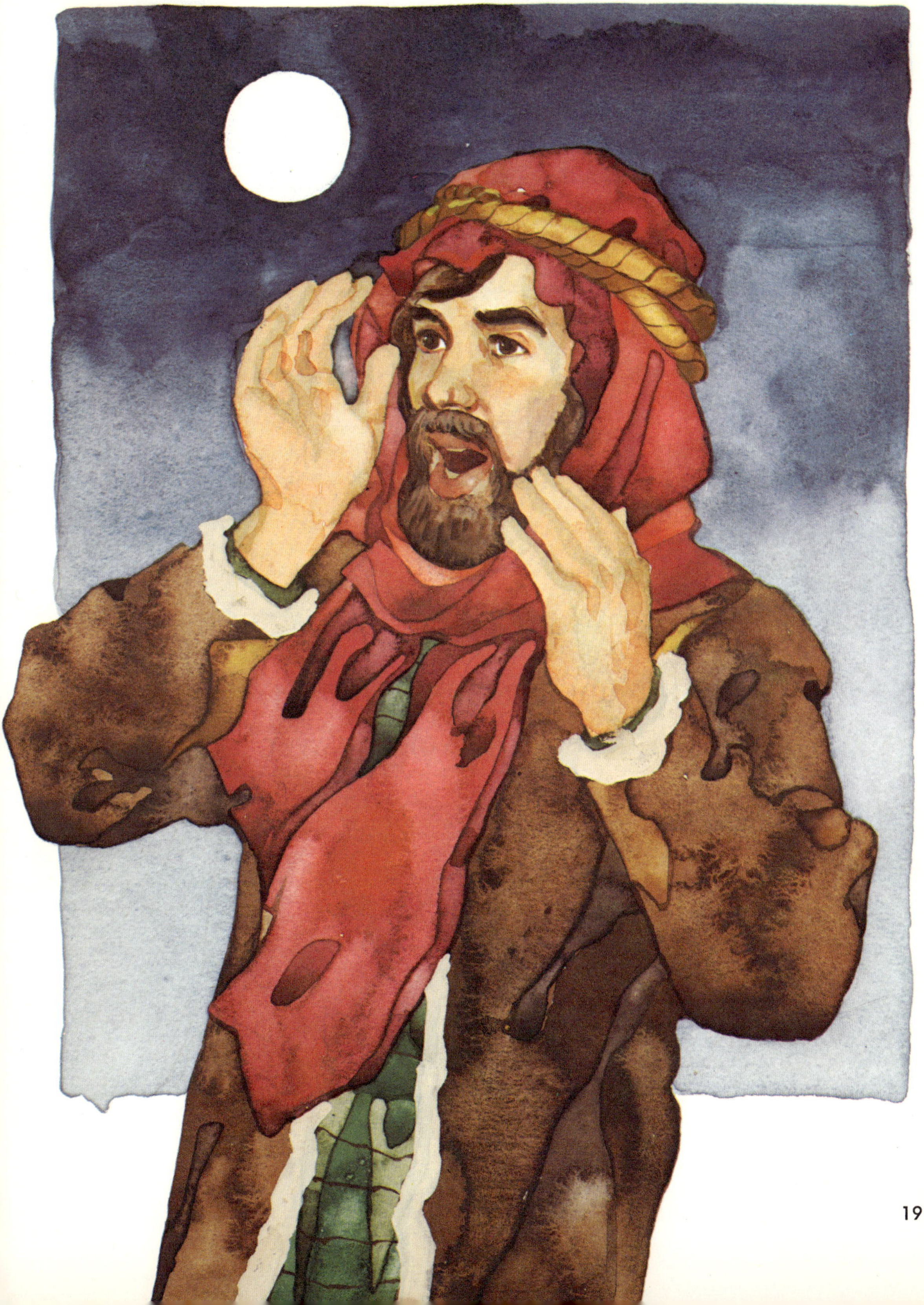

On and on the shepherd walked.
He climbed up the steep hills.

He climbed down the steep hills. The rocks hurt his feet. And he stumbled over the rocks in the darkness. But he kept on calling for his lamb.

Then ... he heard a sound! He stopped and listened. What was it? Listen!

"Baa, baa." He could scarcely hear it. But it must be his little lost lamb! It had to be his little lost lamb!

The shepherd walked toward the sound. Again, he called.

"Baa, baa," came the answer. This time it was louder.

"Oh, my little lost lamb! How glad I am to find you!" said the shepherd, hurrying toward the sound. Yes, it was his lamb. The little lamb was caught in a thorn bush. He was at the very end of a rocky ledge!

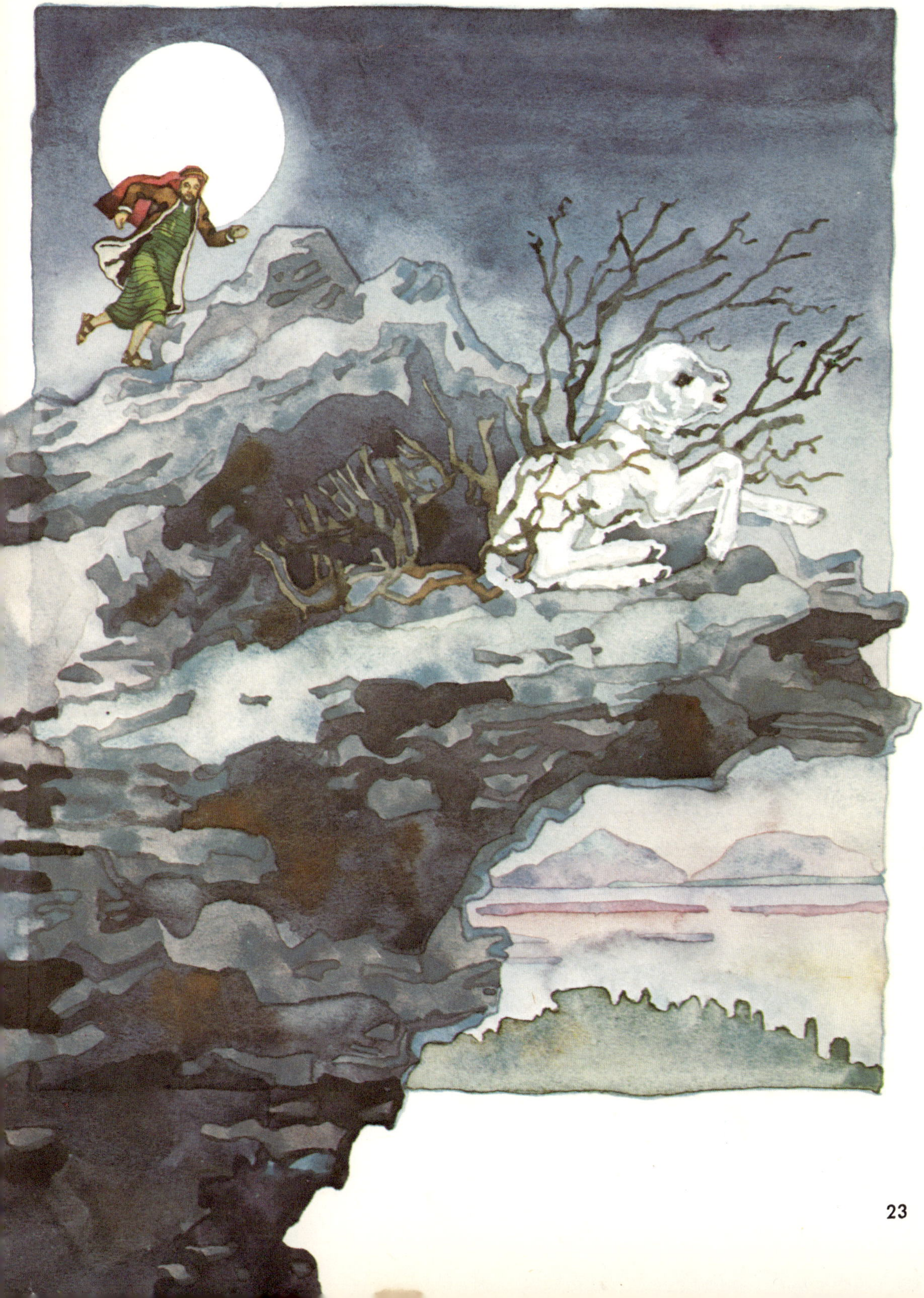

Carefully, the shepherd made his way toward the lamb. Carefully, he moved the thorny branches. Soon the little lamb was free. Then the shepherd moved him to a safer spot. There he took water and cleaned the hurt places. And he put oil on them.

"Baa, baa," said the little lamb. This meant he felt better.

25

Tenderly the shepherd picked up the lamb and held him close. The lamb snuggled against the shepherd's warm body. How glad he was to be found!

He looked up into his shepherd's face. How glad he was to be loved!

Holding the lamb, the shepherd began the long walk back to the sheepfold. Up the steep hill he went. Down the steep hill he went. Over the rocky path, and across the fields.

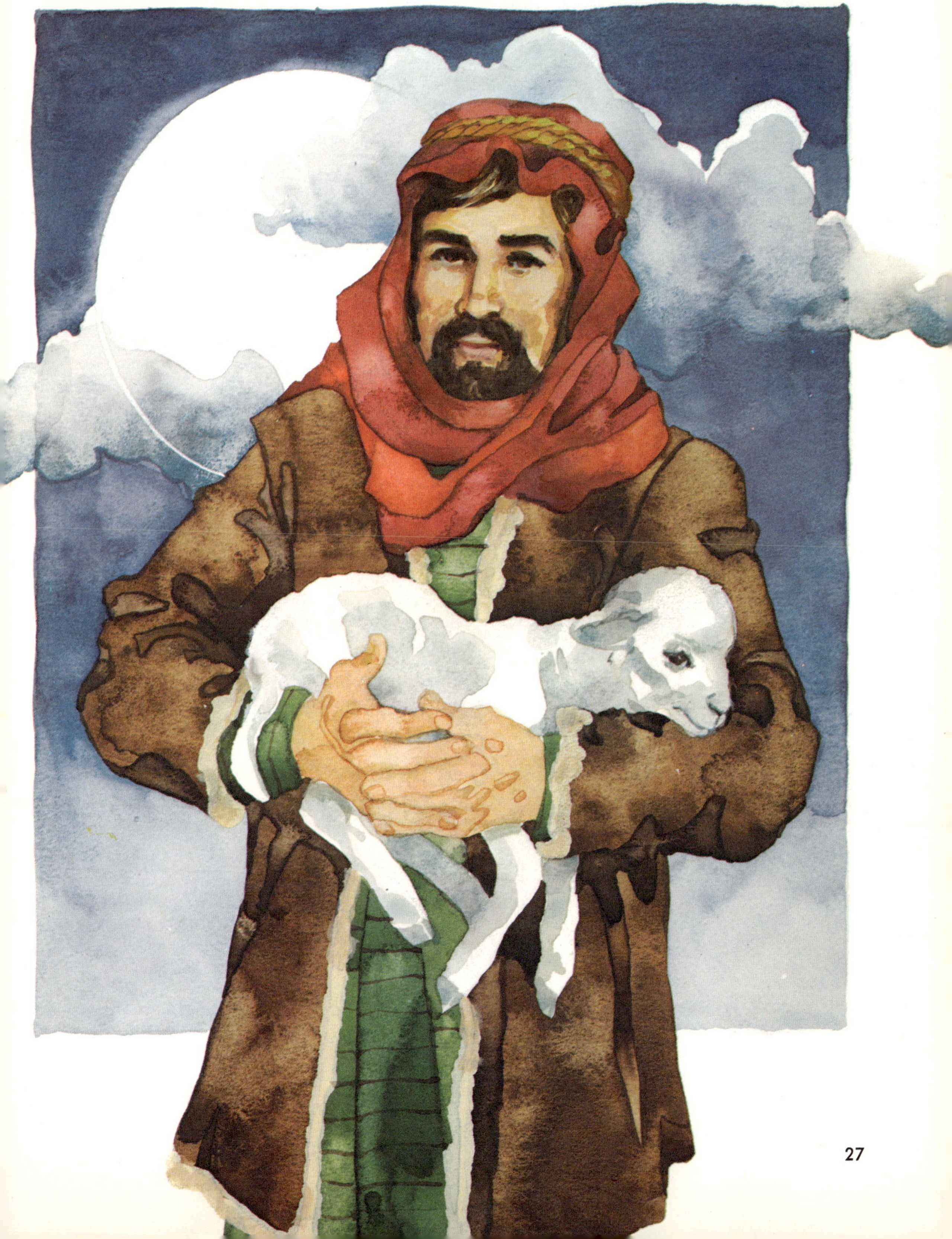

The lamb was heavy, but the shepherd did not mind. He did not mind at all.

At last they came to the sheepfold. The shepherd opened the gate. He put the little lamb down beside his mother.

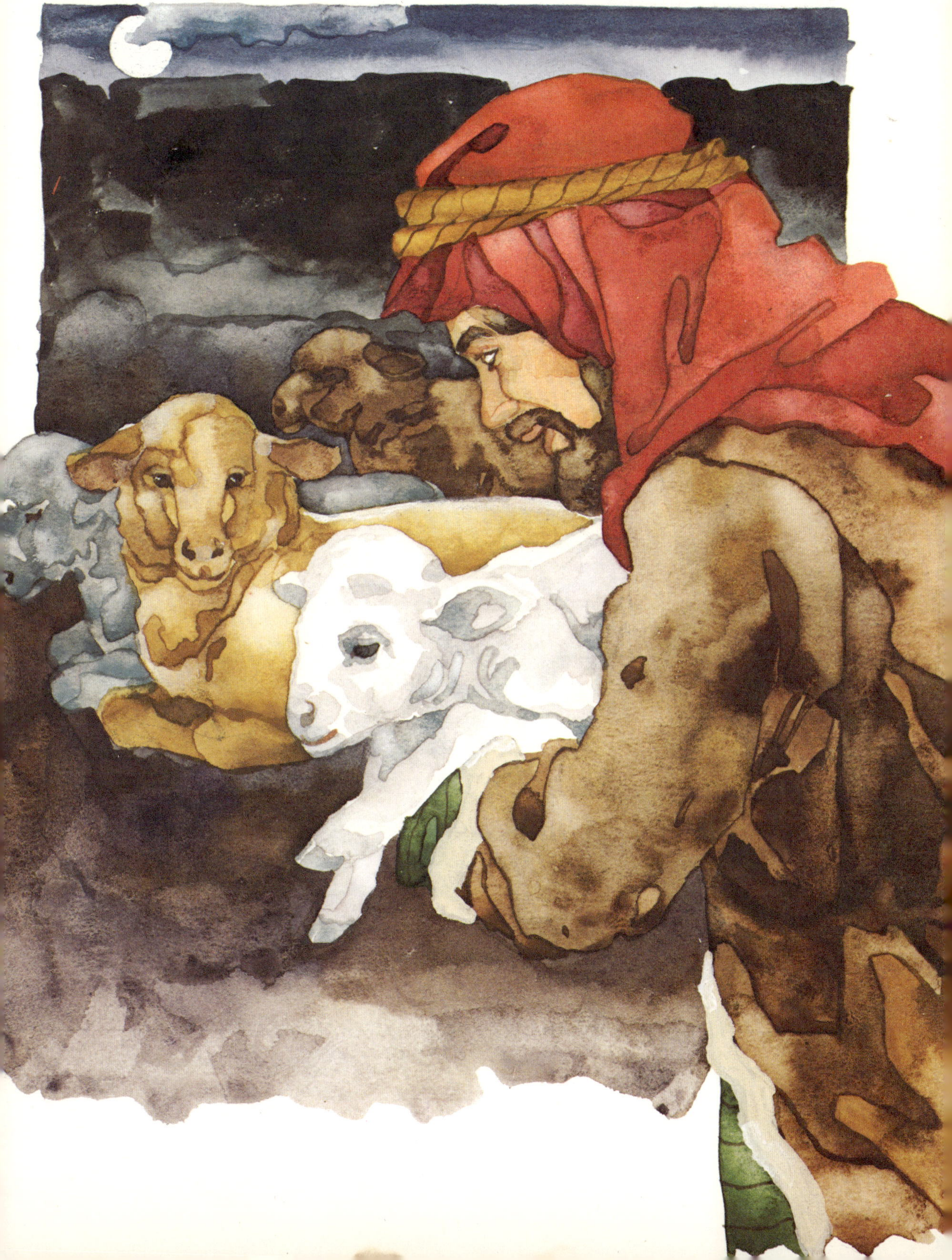

"Baa, baa," said the little lamb.

"Baa, baa," said his mother.

"Baa, baa," said the other sheep. They were glad the lost lamb was safely home.

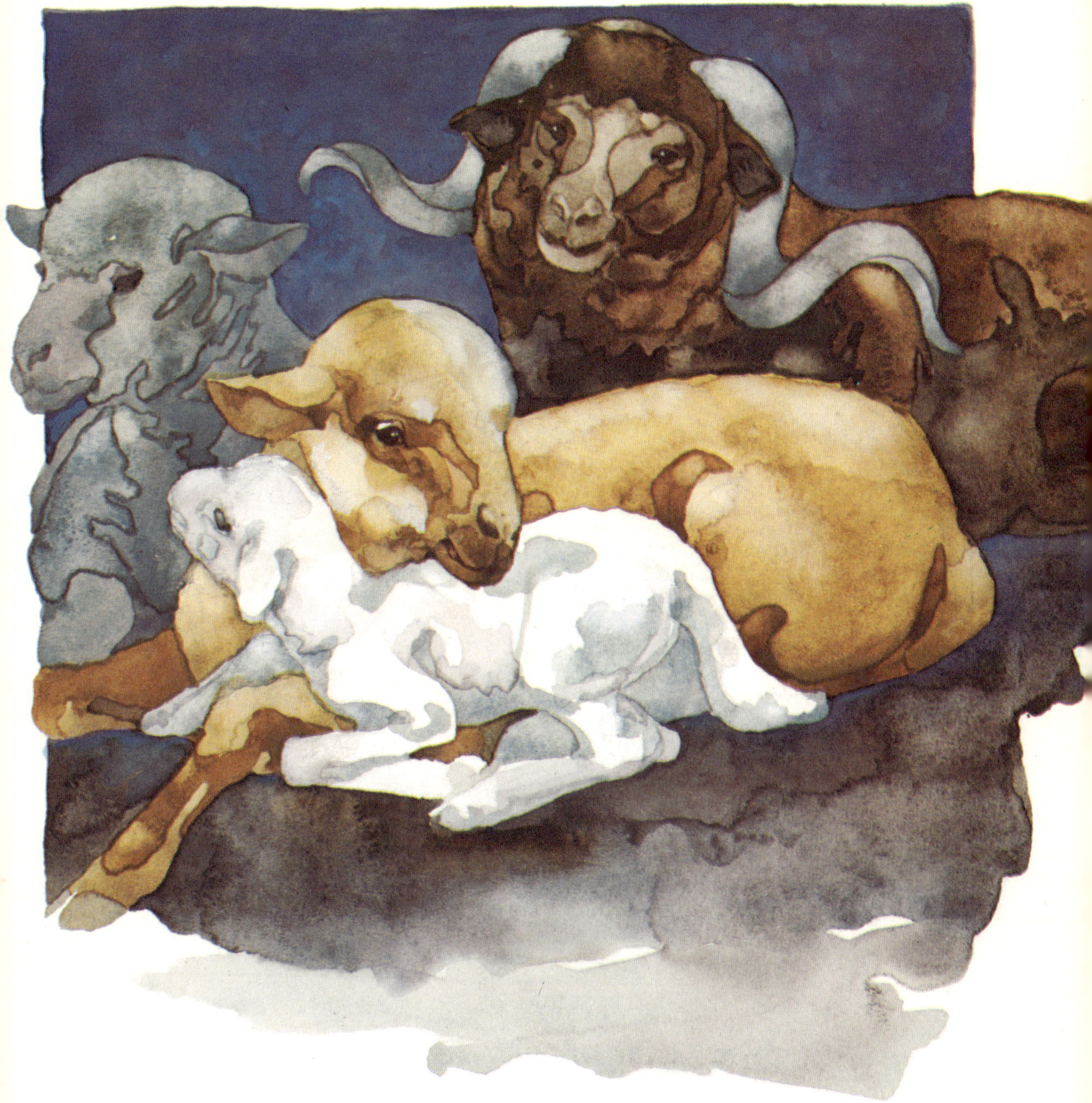

The shepherd was glad too. He went to his house. He called in his neighbors.

"Be happy with me!" he said. "I have found my sheep that was lost!"

MRS PAUL L PREWITT JR
9 STANSBURY CT
FREDERICKSBURG VA 22401

FUMC PRESCHOOL
Box 8469
Fredericksburg, VA 22404